Saudi Arabia

MEGAN KOPP

MEDIA ENHANCED BOOKS
AV2
BY WEIGL™
ADDED VALUE • AUDIO VISUAL

www.av2books.com

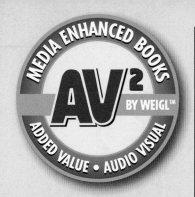

AV² provides enriched content that supplements and complements this book. Weigl's AV² books strive to create inspired learning and engage young minds in a total learning experience.

Your AV² Media Enhanced books come alive with...

Audio
Listen to sections of the book read aloud.

Key Words
Study vocabulary, and complete a matching word activity.

Video
Watch informative video clips.

Quizzes
Test your knowledge.

Go to **www.av2books.com**, and enter this book's unique code.

BOOK CODE

P 8 5 0 8 6 9

Embedded Weblinks
Gain additional information for research.

Slide Show
View images and captions, and prepare a presentation.

AV² by Weigl brings you media enhanced books that support active learning.

Try This!
Complete activities and hands-on experiments.

...and much, much more!

Published by AV² by Weigl
350 5th Avenue, 59th Floor
New York, NY 10118
Websites: www.av2books.com   www.weigl.com

Library of Congress Cataloging-in-Publication Data

Kopp, Megan.
 Saudi Arabia / Megan Kopp.
    pages cm. — (Exploring countries)
 Includes index.
 ISBN 978-1-4896-1026-3 (hardcover : alk. paper) — ISBN 978-1-4896-1027-0 (softcover : alk. paper) —
 ISBN 978-1-4896-1028-7 (single user ebk.) — ISBN 978-1-4896-1029-4 (multi user ebk.)
 1. Saudi Arabia—Juvenile literature. I. Title.
 DS204.25.K67 2014
 953.8—dc23
                        2014005945

Printed in the United States of America in North Mankato, Minnesota
1 2 3 4 5 6 7 8 9 0 18 17 16 15 14

042014
WEP150314

Project Coordinator Heather Kissock
Art Director Terry Paulhus

Photo Credits
Every reasonable effort has been made to trace ownership and to obtain permission to reprint copyright material. The publishers would be pleased to have any errors or omissions brought to their attention so that they may be corrected in subsequent printings.

Weigl acknowledges Getty Images as its primary image supplier for this title.

Contents

Saudi Arabia Overview

Saudi Arabia is the largest country in the Arabian Peninsula. This peninsula is located in the Middle East, a region in western Asia and North Africa. Vast deserts cover almost all of Saudi Arabia. The country is the birthplace of Islam, the religion followed by Muslims, and some of the most important Islamic holy sites are found in Saudi Arabia. The country has also been home to **indigenous** peoples who have lived on the land for thousands of years. Camel caravans carried goods across the deserts, stopping at **oases** for food, water, and shelter. Today, Saudi Arabia is a **monarchy**, ruled by a large royal family. Wealth from vast deposits of oil and natural gas has helped to modernize the country, but traditional ways are still important to the Saudi people.

Dances are performed at the Jinādiriyyah Heritage and Cultural Festival, which attracts more than 1 million visitors each year.

On Saudi National Day, September 23, children wave the country's flag and dress in green, a color important to Muslims.

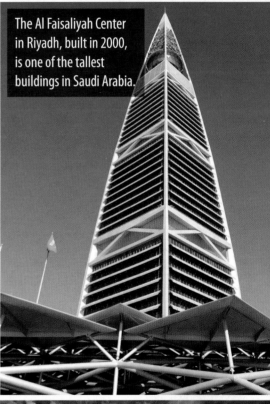

The Al Faisaliyah Center in Riyadh, built in 2000, is one of the tallest buildings in Saudi Arabia.

Drilling platforms are a common sight in Saudi Arabia. Oil is the country's most important product.

There are an estimated 1 million camels in Saudi Arabia. They are common in the deserts but are seen elsewhere as well.

Exploring
Saudi Arabia

Saudi Arabia covers about four-fifths of the Arabian Peninsula. The Red Sea, which is to the west, separates Saudi Arabia from Africa. Jordan, Iraq, and Kuwait share borders with Saudi Arabia in the north. The Persian Gulf lies to the east, and Qatar, the United Arab Emirates (UAE), Oman, and Yemen share borders to the south and southeast. Saudi Arabia is the largest country in the Middle East.

Jordan

Najd

SAUDI

Najd

Egypt

N

Red Sea

Asir Mountains

Sudan

Asir Mountains

Map Legend

 Saudi Arabia   Najd   📍 Capital City

Land   Asir Mountains

Water   Rubʿ al-Khali

SCALE   500 Miles

500 Kilometers

Asir Mountains

The Asir Mountains are located in the southwest. The region also contains plains and valleys. The area gets more rain than much of the country. Deposits of nickel, copper, and zinc are found there.

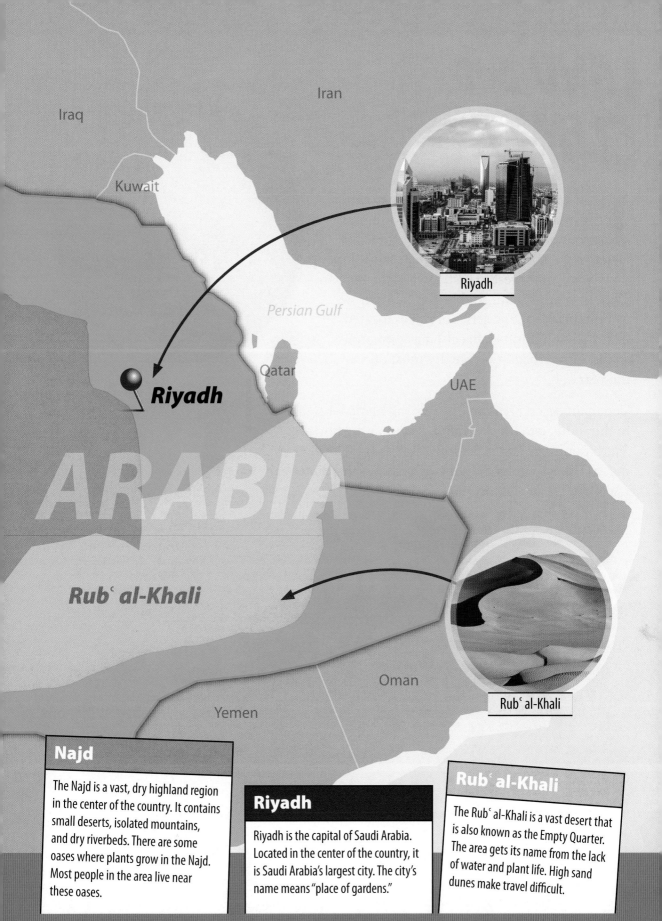

Iran

Iraq

Kuwait

Riyadh

Persian Gulf

Qatar

UAE

Riyadh

ARABIA

Rub᷍ al-Khali

Oman

Rub᷍ al-Khali

Yemen

Najd

The Najd is a vast, dry highland region in the center of the country. It contains small deserts, isolated mountains, and dry riverbeds. There are some oases where plants grow in the Najd. Most people in the area live near these oases.

Riyadh

Riyadh is the capital of Saudi Arabia. Located in the center of the country, it is Saudi Arabia's largest city. The city's name means "place of gardens."

Rub᷍ al-Khali

The Rub᷍ al-Khali is a vast desert that is also known as the Empty Quarter. The area gets its name from the lack of water and plant life. High sand dunes make travel difficult.

LAND AND CLIMATE

In western Saudi Arabia, a rocky **plateau** rises sharply from the Red Sea. Mountain ranges near the western coast include the Hejaz in the north and the Asir. The land slopes downward from west to east, toward the Persian Gulf. In central Saudi Arabia, the Tuwayq Mountains are a long series of ridges located near Riyadh. Saudi Arabia also has numerous wadis, or riverbeds, that are dry most of the year.

The main desert areas are the Rubʿ al-Khali, located in the south, and the Al-Nafūd, found in the north. Sand mountains in the Rubʿ al-Khali soar 800 feet (245 meters) above sea level. In the Al-Nafūd, sand dunes can rise higher than 100 feet (30 m).

Dust storms and sandstorms are common in many areas of Saudi Arabia.

Except for wadis, Saudi Arabia has no permanent rivers or lakes. Small canals have been dug near wells to bring water to farm fields. The country's oases vary in size. Some are quite small, but others cover a number of square miles (square kilometers).

Saudi Arabia's climate is extremely hot and dry. June to August are the warmest months, when daytime temperatures soar above 100° Fahrenheit (38° Celsius) in most of the country. In some places in the desert, the temperature can be higher than 130° F (54° C). The winter months, from December to February, are the coolest. Average temperatures are 74° F (23° C) in the city of Jiddah, 63° F (17° C) in Al-Dammām, and 58° F (14° C) in Riyadh. During the winter, the temperature can sometimes drop to below freezing in the mountains.

Rainfall is seasonal in Saudi Arabia. Heavy rains usually occur in March and April, and there can be little or no rain for the rest of the year. Average rainfall across the country is 2 to 3 inches (5 to 7.5 centimeters) a year, although some places get more. The Rubʿ al-Khali, however, can go 10 years without seeing a drop of rain.

Land and Climate BY THE NUMBERS

830,000
Total area of Saudi Arabia in square miles. (2,149,690 sq. km)

250,000 SQUARE MILES
Size of the Rubʿ al-Khali, which is the world's largest sand desert. (647,500 sq. km)

19 Inches
Annual rainfall in the Asir Mountains. (48 cm)

10,279 feet
Height of Mount Sawdāʾ, the highest point in Saudi Arabia, which is located near the city of Abhā in the south. (3,133 m)

Wadis fill with water during the months of the year when there are heavy rains.

PLANTS AND ANIMALS

Even though most of Saudi Arabia is desert, there are more than 2,000 **species** of plants in the country. About 40 of these are found nowhere else in the world. Most of the plants that grow in Saudi Arabia are small herbs and shrubs that need little water. Most trees, such as the plentiful date palm, grow around oases that have enough water to support their growth. At high elevations, especially during the rainy season, wildflowers grow.

About 80 species of mammals live in Saudi Arabia. They include camels, wolves, hyenas, jackals, foxes, mongooses, porcupines, hares, gazelles, baboons, honey badgers, hedgehogs, sand rats, and jerboas. Wild goats called ibex live in the mountains. The Arabian oryx, which is a type of antelope, became **extinct** in nature in the 1970s. Some oryx bred in zoos have been placed in nature reserves.

Many different kinds of birds live year-round in Saudi Arabia, and hundreds of other types **migrate** through the country. Species of birds found only in Saudi Arabia include two types of partridge, the South Arabian wheatear, the Arabian woodpecker, and the Arabian waxbill. Flamingos, pelicans, egrets, eagles, vultures, owls, crows, ravens, and sparrows are all common.

Arabian camels, also called dromedaries, have one hump. It stores fat, which is converted into water and energy when needed.

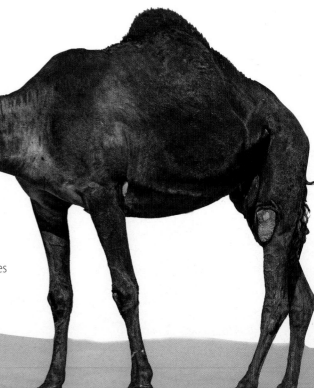

Plants and Animals BY THE NUMBERS

432
Number of bird species in Saudi Arabia.

1950s
Years when hunting from vehicles greatly reduced the populations of many types of large animals, such as the oryx, leopard, and ibex.

7
Number of species of **amphibians** found in Saudi Arabia.

NATURAL RESOURCES

Petroleum, or oil, is Saudi Arabia's most valuable natural resource. The country ranks first in the world for **oil reserves**, with more than 260 billion barrels (31 billion kiloliters). Oil deposits are located mostly in the eastern part of the country and under the coastal waters of the Persian Gulf. Saudi Arabia also has about 4 percent of the world's reserves of natural gas.

Deposits of many kinds of minerals are found in the country. Gold, silver, and copper have been taken from the Mahd Al-Dhahab mine in western Saudi Arabia since 1000 BC. Gold is also mined at Shukhaybirat, Al Hajar, Bi'r At Tawilah, and Al Amar. Other mineral resources include zinc, lead, iron, tungsten, nickel, chrome, and bauxite. There are large gypsum deposits near Yanbu.

Water is a scarce resource in Saudi Arabia. Aquifers, or underground water reservoirs, found in the eastern part of the country provide some drinking water. Saudi Arabia has the largest **desalination** program in the world to provide water for homes and businesses.

Natural Resources BY THE NUMBERS

18% Portion of the world's oil reserves that are in Saudi Arabia.

8 million Number of barrels of oil produced each day in Saudi Arabia. (1.3 million kl)

70% Portion of the water used in Saudi Arabian cities that comes from desalination.

Saudi Arabia has about 100 major oil and gas fields, where these resources are pumped from beneath the ground.

TOURISM

Saudi Arabia is a country rich in history and culture, but until recently tourism has not been a major business. Most visitors to the kingdom are Muslims making the hajj, a religious **pilgrimage** to the city of Mecca. For many years, non-Muslims had difficulty gaining permission to enter the country.

In 2000, the Saudi Commission for Tourism was established to promote tourism in the kingdom. The name was changed to the Saudi Commission for Tourism and **Antiquities** in 2008. Since then, the government has made it easier for tourists to get **visas**.

The Saudi government is also investing in the business of tourism. Money is being spent on advertising to make people aware of the country's attractions. Museums and hotels are being built. Airports are being expanded. More than 1 million citizens had tourism-related jobs in 2013.

Hundreds of sculptures can be found throughout the streets of Jiddah.

Muhammad is buried in the Prophet's Mosque, located in Medina. This mosque, or Muslim house of worship, can hold 500,000 people.

Riyadh has many cultural attractions. Qasr Al-Hokm, the oldest section of the city, has many historic buildings from the 1800s and early 1900s. Riyadh's historic buildings include the Mismāk fortress. The fort played a major role in the formation of the modern kingdom of Saudi Arabia when it was captured in 1902 by King ʿAbd al-ʿAzīz, also known as Ibn Saʿūd. The National Museum and the Al Murabba Palace in Riyadh are now part of the King ʿAbd al-ʿAzīz Historical Center.

Located on the Red Sea, Jiddah is Saudi Arabia's second-largest city. Attractions in the older part of the city include the souks, or markets, and historic homes made of coral. Jiddah has hundreds of gardens.

Visitors to the Jiddah area can also enjoy diving, sailing, and other water sports. The Asir region is farther south along the Red Sea coast. It has steep mountains, lush greenery, and cool breezes.

The holy city of Mecca is the birthplace of Muhammad, the founder of Islam. The Great Mosque of Mecca houses Islam's most sacred shrine, the Kaʿbah. Medina is the second major holy city of Islam. The city's Prophet's Mosque is on the site of a mosque first built by Muhammad.

ALMOST 3.2 MILLION
Number of pilgrims who made the hajj in 2012, including about 1.7 million people from outside Saudi Arabia.

1.1 Million Number of acres in Asir National Park, the first national park established in Saudi Arabia. (445,000 hectares)

Madain Saleh, in central Saudi Arabia, is called the "capital of monuments." It contains well-preserved remains of ancient cultures, including large tombs cut into the rock.

INDUSTRY

Petroleum was discovered in Saudi Arabia in 1938. However, it was not until after the end of World War II in 1945 that the oil industry began to boom. The Arabian American Oil Company, also called Aramco, opened a pipeline in 1950. For more than 30 years, it carried Saudi oil west to ports in Lebanon on the Mediterranean Sea. From there, the oil was shipped to Europe and North America. Another pipeline, called Petroline, opened in 1981. It carries crude oil from eastern Saudi Arabia and the Persian Gulf west to the Red Sea.

Also by the early 1980s, the Saudi government took complete control of Aramco, which had been owned by several U.S. oil companies. Aramco was later renamed Saudi Aramco. Today, the oil industry remains the most important industry in the country.

Manufacturing has grown in recent decades. In 1976, the government established the Saudi Arabian Basic Industries Corporation. Its goal was to encourage the development of various industries. Goods manufactured in the country include steel, copper, and aluminum products. **Petrochemicals**, fertilizers, truck parts, ammonia, soap, and cement are also produced.

$921.7 Billion
Size of Saudi Arabia's **GDP**.

1951
Year Aramco made the first discovery in the Middle East of an offshore petroleum deposit, located in the Persian Gulf.

More Than $300 Billion
Amount of money Saudi Arabia receives each year from selling oil to other countries.

Large petrochemical factories are located in Jubail on the Persian Gulf and Yanbu on the Red Sea.

Saudi Arabia had established 14 "industrial cities" as of 2013. These sites have such facilities as factories, schools to train workers, desalination plants, and seaports. Jubail and Yanbu are among the locations with industrial cities.

GOODS AND SERVICES

8 MILLION
Number of workers in Saudi Arabia.

Before the discovery of oil in the 1930s, Saudi Arabia was an agricultural society. Many people were **nomads**. They raised camels, sheep, and goats, and they moved from place to place to find food and water for their animals. Crops were grown where the soil was suitable and there was enough water. Most agricultural products were used locally, although a few crops were sold to other countries. People also earned money by providing goods and services to pilgrims coming to Mecca and Medina.

LESS THAN 2%
Portion of Saudi Arabia's land that is used to grow crops.

Oil changed everything. After World War II, the government used money received from selling oil to build roads, airports, seaports, schools, and hospitals. Service industries grew rapidly. These are industries in which workers provide a service to other people, rather than produce goods. Service workers include people employed in government offices, schools, stores, banks, and hotels.

Government desalination and **irrigation** projects made water available for farming in areas that used to be too dry for agriculture. The kingdom now produces all the wheat, eggs, and milk it needs, although it still **imports** most of the food it uses. Wheat is the largest grain crop. In addition, dates, melons, tomatoes, potatoes, cucumbers, pumpkins, citrus fruits, and squash are grown.

More Than 31,000
Number of doctors in Saudi Arabia.

Saudi Arabia has a modern health care system, and people receive free health care. The infant **mortality rate** has dropped sharply in recent decades. **Life expectancy** has increased.

About 500,000 tons (455,000 tonnes) of dates are grown in Saudi Arabia each year. Much of the crop is donated to international food aid groups.

INDIGENOUS PEOPLES

Scientists have found evidence that nomadic groups of hunter-gatherers were living in the area of the Arabian Peninsula as far back as 15,000 to 20,000 years ago. These people hunted animals and gathered parts of plants for food. Ancient petroglyphs, or rock carvings, have been found throughout what is now Saudi Arabia.

The climate became very dry about 15,000 years ago, and people were forced to move into mountain valleys and oases, where water could be found. Most Saudi Arabians today are **descendants** of these people who settled near oases. They are part of the Arab cultural group.

About 5 to 10 percent of the Saudi Arabian population today is made up of Bedouins. Bedouins are nomadic. For centuries, they have roamed the great deserts of Saudi Arabia with their herds of animals. They migrate into the deserts during the rainy season and move back to settled areas in the dry summer months.

1,500 Number of sites in Saudi Arabia that have petroglyphs.

ABOUT 90% Percentage of the Saudi population that is Arab.

1 Million Years Old
Age of stone tools found in the **archaeological** site of Shuwayhitiyah in Saudi Arabia.

Traditional Bedouin society is **patriarchal**. The male head of a large family or tribe is called the sheikh. The sheikh is assisted by a tribal council made up of older men.

Bedouins place great value on cooperation, responsibility, and loyalty to their group.

THE AGE OF EXPLORATION

Trade was important to the Arabian Peninsula's development. Huge camel caravans from what is now Oman and Yemen traveled northwest across present-day Saudi Arabia carrying agricultural goods such as almonds, dates, and spices. The caravans passed through Mecca and Medina, eventually arriving in cities north of the peninsula.

The introduction of Islam in the 7th century AD further defined the region's culture. Within a century of its birth in Saudi Arabia, Islam had spread west across North Africa and east as far as India and China. The religion's growth led to a period of major advances in science, philosophy, and the arts known as the Islamic Golden Age. When Muslim pilgrims from around the world traveled to the holy sites in Mecca and Medina, they also enriched the region's culture.

Beginning in the 1500s, the Ottoman Turks gained control of a large part of the Arabian Peninsula, which became part of the Ottoman Empire. During World War I, Arabs under Ibn Saʿūd and other leaders won back their land from the Ottoman Turks. They were helped by T. E. Lawrence. He was a British soldier who became known as Lawrence of Arabia.

Arabic books from hundreds of years ago included drawings of the Kaʿbah. This building is located at the center of the Great Mosque in Mecca.

EARLY SETTLERS

The area that is now Saudi Arabia was divided into four traditional regions. These areas are the Al-Hijāz, Asir, Najd, and Al-Hasa. Many trade routes passed through the Al-Hijāz and Najd regions. Settlements developed along these caravan routes, where local people could provide water and shelter to the traders in exchange for some of their goods. With the rise of Islam, religious pilgrims began following the same trade routes to reach Mecca and Medina.

Muslims gathered in cities around the world to travel together to Mecca.

A world atlas created during the 1500s included maps of Saudi Arabia and the surrounding region.

Tabūk, Taymā', Linah, and Hai'l were trade settlements established between the Najd and Egypt. Other settlements developed in parts of the Najd that had good land for growing crops and a source of water. The Al-Hijāz, in the western part of the country, is where Mecca and Medina developed, as well as the port city of Jiddah.

In the Asir region, cooler temperatures and access to water led to the creation of agricultural settlements. Trading centers also developed. During the 19th century, the Asir region was one of the most heavily populated areas of what is now Saudi Arabia.

Al-Hasa is in the east, along the Persian Gulf. It has large oases, and many early settlers in this region were involved in agriculture. Another traditional industry in coastal areas was diving for pearls, which grew inside some oysters living in the Persian Gulf.

1600s
Years when Riyadh developed as a small village, on the site of an earlier settlement.

20,000
Population of Al-Hasa in 1865.

1902 to 1932
Years when the Najd was an independent kingdom.

Less Than 200
Number of families living in the trade settlements of Tabūk, Taymā', Linah, and Hai'l in 1845.

Archaeological remains of ancient kingdoms can be found in Al Ula in northwest Saudi Arabia, located on a major trade route.

POPULATION

Saudi Arabia has a population of 26.9 million people. On average, there are about 32.5 people per square mile of land (12.5 per sq. km). The average for the United States is 89 people per square mile (34 per sq. km).

Until the second half of the 20th century, most of the population did not live in cities. Mecca was the largest city in the country in the 1940s, with only 80,000 people. After oil was discovered, large **urban** centers developed to support oil-related activities and other new industries.

Today, more than 82 percent of the people live in cities and their surrounding areas. Riyadh has a population of 5.5 million, and 3.6 million people live in Jiddah. Mecca now has a population of 1.6 million people, while Medina has 1.1 million.

In addition to native-born Saudi Arabians, millions of foreign workers live in the kingdom. They come from Arab countries in the Middle East and many other areas of the world. Most foreign workers do not settle in Saudi Arabia permanently, but many stay for a number of years.

Government policies promote large families. The country's birth rate, the number of births per thousand people, is high compared to many other countries. The population is young. Almost two-thirds of the people are under the age of 30.

750,000 Current population of the once small fishing village of Al-Dammām.

More Than 8 Million
Number of foreign residents in Saudi Arabia.

28% Portion of the population that is less than 15 years old.

The Kingdom Centre building in Riyadh was completed in 2002, when the city was growing rapidly.

POLITICS AND GOVERNMENT

On September 23, 1932, the kingdom of Saudi Arabia was established by Ibn Saʾūd. The king, who was the country's first monarch, died in 1953. Since then, the royal Saʾūd family has ruled the country. There are thousands of princes from different branches of the family. Each king is chosen from among these princes.

Saudi Arabia has no written **constitution** and no elected legislature. There are no political parties. It is an Islamic state based on principles of the Qurʾān, which is Islam's holy book, and Islamic law.

In 1992, King Fahd issued a document known as the Basic Law of Government. It provides guidelines for how the government is run. It also describes the rights and responsibilities of citizens.

The king appoints a Council of Ministers. The ministers advise the king. They are also responsible for government policy in areas such as finance, defense, education, and health. Decisions are made through agreement among the members of the royal family. The views of religious scholars, tribal sheikhs, and heads of important business families are also considered.

Elections for local officials in Saudi Arabia have been held since 1939. In the 2015 elections, women will be allowed to vote for the first time.

2005
Year ʿAbd Allāh ibn ʿAbd al-ʿAzīz became the king, following the death of his brother, King Fahd.

22,000
Number of members of the royal family in 2010.

CULTURAL GROUPS

Compared to many other countries, the society of Saudi Arabia is not diverse. Almost all Saudis are Arab. The largest groups of foreign workers who have come into the country in recent decades are from Yemen, Egypt, Palestine, Syria, Iraq, South Korea, and the Philippines. Some Europeans and North Americans have moved to the kingdom for specialized technical jobs.

Strong, hot coffee is a traditional beverage enjoyed by Saudis both at home and in coffeehouses.

Arabic is the country's official language. Three main dialects, or variations, are spoken in Saudi Arabia. This means that the language is slightly different in the eastern, central, and western parts of the country. Some foreign workers speak various dialects of Arabic from other regions. Foreign workers also speak numerous non-Arabic languages, such as Persian, Urdu, Pashto, Tagalog, and Korean. Many Saudis understand English.

Shopping in Riyadh's souks is a popular pastime.

Islam is the official religion of Saudi Arabia. It has two main branches, Sunni and Shīʿite. Most Saudi Arabians follow the Sunni branch of Islam. Shīʿites are found mainly in eastern Saudi Arabia.

Saudi society has strict rules on many types of behavior and forms of dress. Drinking alcohol is forbidden, and there are no movie theaters or public showings of films. Publicly expressing opinions about current issues is not encouraged. Workers are not allowed to join labor unions.

Most Saudis dress in traditional clothing. Men wear long white robes and pants. They also wear a head covering called a kaffiyeh. It is held in place by a cord that is often made of camel hair. Women wear a loose top over pants. In public, they are expected to wear long black cloaks. They also cover their heads, and sometimes their faces, with scarves and veils.

Women are not allowed to drive in Saudi Arabia. A woman or girl has a male guardian, who may be a father, husband, brother, or other family member. Often, a woman needs the approval of her male guardian for such activities as opening a bank account, attending college, or taking a job.

The black cloak worn by Saudi women is called an abaya, while the scraf worn around the head is called a shayla.

ARTS AND ENTERTAINMENT

Poetry has long been an important part of traditional Saudi Arabian culture. For desert nomads, storytelling was an oral tradition. Through stories and poems, they shared tales of love, war, and historic events.

Saudis have also always enjoyed music and dance. Traditional songs usually come from poetry and are sung by a group. Instruments include the rabābah, which is similar to a three-stringed fiddle, and percussion instruments such as drums and tambourines.

For hundreds of years, **calligraphy** has played a significant role in Saudi culture. It has historically been used for religious purposes, such as writing the Qur'ān. Calligraphy is found not only on paper, but also on metalwork, ceramics, glass, fabrics, paintings, and sculptures. Examples of calligraphy are often found on the interior walls of mosques, offices, and homes. Museums collect rare manuscripts showing calligraphy. Today, organizations provide training in the art form and hold competitions to encourage new artists.

One of the main streets of Jiddah is decorated by a statue of Arabic calligraphy.

Saudi poets read their works and sign copies of their books at public events. They also take part in a competition that appears on television.

Geometric and floral designs are commonly found throughout Saudi Arabia's visual arts. For thousands of years, artists worked with ancient designs. With the rapid changes in society following the discovery of oil, there has been increased exposure to outside influences.

Jewelry has long been a key part of Arabian dress. Jewelry was used for personal decoration and to show social and economic status. Traditional jewelry was most often made of silver. Pieces also featured turquoise, garnets, and amber from the country's mines, as well as pearls and coral from coastal areas. Tiny bells, coins, and chains were often used for decoration. Designs featured complex patterns of geometric shapes, leaves, crescents, and flowers.

One of the best-known cultural events in Saudi Arabia is the Jinādiriyyah Heritage and Cultural Festival. The two-week festival is organized every year by the National Guard in Riyadh. Potters, woodworkers, and weavers demonstrate their traditional crafts. There are also metalsmiths, who create traditional brass and copper pots, and basketweavers, who turn palm fronds and straw into hats, baskets, and containers decorated with colorful designs. Potters use foot-powered wheels to shape clay bowls and water jars. Singers and dancers perform traditional music.

A traditional military-style dance, called the ʿardah, is performed by lines of men with swords. They dance to the beat of drums and tambourines.

SPORTS

Saudi Arabia's most popular sporting events revolve around racing. Horse races have been held in the kingdom for centuries. Today, there are racetracks in Riyadh and other cities.

Camel racing is a traditional sport among the Bedouins. In the past, thousands of camels would race across the open desert. There are now modern racetracks, and camel races are held weekly during the cooler months at Riyadh Stadium. In addition, about 2,000 camels and riders compete in the King's Cup Camel Race every year in Riyadh.

Other traditional sports include falconry, in which small animals are hunted by birds of prey such as falcons. Falconry in Saudi Arabia is limited in order to protect game animals from overhunting. Popular modern sports include soccer, basketball, and other ball games.

Falconry may have begun as a way to hunt food, but over the years it developed into a popular sport.

Most competitors in the King's Cup Camel Race are boys who have trained in camel racing from a young age.

The government has encouraged sports by building large facilities called sports cities in major urban areas. Each sports city has indoor and outdoor stadiums, an Olympic-size swimming pool, playgrounds, and a sports medicine clinic. Neighborhood sports facilities have also been built.

Since the early 1970s, Saudi athletes have represented the kingdom in international competitions. Saudi Arabia first participated in the Summer Olympic Games in 1972. In 2012, for the first time, Saudi women competed in the Olympics.

The Saudi national soccer team has had much international success. The team qualified for its first appearance in the Olympics in 1984. The national team has qualified for the men's World Cup four times beginning in 1994, and it has won the Asian Cup three times.

Saudi Arabia is home to several Little League baseball teams. The Arabian-American Little League team of Dhahran has qualified for the Little League Baseball World Series in Williamsport, Pennsylvania. Saudis also enjoy scuba diving, windsurfing, and sailing.

Saudi Arabia has a number of golf courses. Americans working in the kingdom introduced golf in the late 1940s when they created a course in the sand near Dhahran. They did not create greens around the holes, since it was difficult to grow grass. Instead, they mixed oil with the sand and then played on the "browns."

Sarah Attar competed in the 2012 Olympics, one of the first two Saudi women to do so.

Sports BY THE NUMBERS

1964 Year the Saudi Arabian Olympic Committee was organized.

2000

Year that Hadi Souan Somayli won a silver medal in the 400-meter hurdles in the Summer Games, the kingdom's first Olympic medal.

2010 Year that equestrian Dalma Malhas, the first woman to represent the kingdom in an international competition, won a bronze medal in show jumping at the Youth Olympic Games.

Mapping Saudi Arabia

We use many tools to interpret maps and to understand the locations of features such as cities, states, oases, and deserts. The map below has many tools to help interpret information on the map of Saudi Arabia.

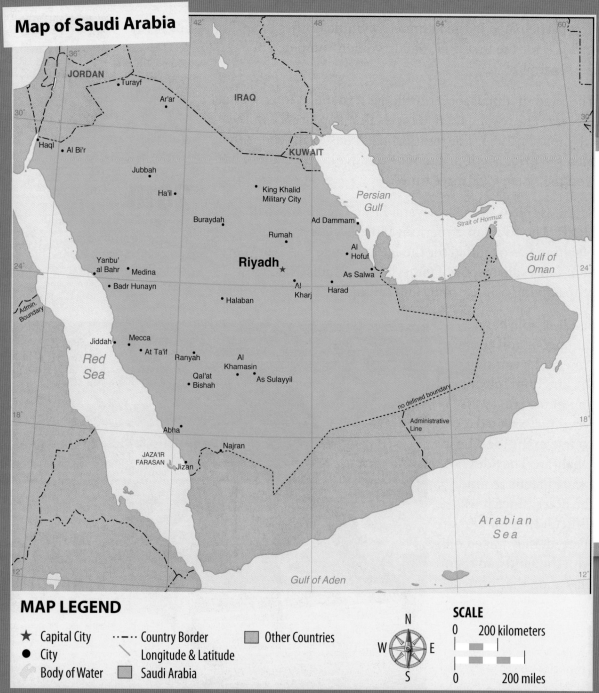

Map of Saudi Arabia

JORDAN
Turayf
Ar'ar
IRAQ
Haql
Al Bi'r
KUWAIT
Jubbah
Ha'il
King Khalid Military City
Persian Gulf
Buraydah
Ad Dammam
Strait of Hormuz
Rumah
Al Hofuf
Gulf of Oman
Yanbu' al Bahr
Medina
Riyadh ★
As Salwa
Badr Hunayn
Al Kharj
Harad
Admin. Boundary
Halaban
Jiddah
Mecca
At Ta'if
Ranyah
Al Khamasin
Red Sea
Qal'at Bishah
As Sulayyil
no defined boundary
Abha
Administrative Line
JAZA'IR FARASAN
Najran
Jizan
Arabian Sea
Gulf of Aden

MAP LEGEND

★ Capital City
● City
Body of Water
---·--- Country Border
Longitude & Latitude
Saudi Arabia
Other Countries

SCALE
0   200 kilometers
0   200 miles

N W E S

Mapping Tools

- The compass rose shows north, south, east, and west. The points in between represent northeast, northwest, southeast, and southwest.
- The map scale shows that the distances on a map represent much longer distances in real life. If you measure the distance between objects on a map, you can use the map scale to calculate the actual distance in miles or kilometers between those two points.

- The lines of latitude and longitude are long lines that appear on maps. The lines of latitude run east to west and measure how far north or south of the equator a place is located. The lines of longitude run north to south and measure how far east or west of the Prime Meridian a place is located. A location on a map can be found by using two numbers where latitude and longitude meet. This number is called a coordinate and is written using degrees and direction. For example, the city of Riyadh would be found at 25°N and 47°E on a map.

Map It!

Using the map and the appropriate tools, complete the activities below.

Locating with latitude and longitude
1. Which city is found at approximately 24°N and 49°E?
2. Name the body of water found at 26°N and 50°E.
3. Which city is found on the map at about 18°N and 42°E?

Distances between points
4. Using the map scale and a ruler, calculate the approximate distance between the cities of Mecca and Riyadh.
5. Measuring across the country, what is the approximate width of Saudi Arabia from the Red Sea in the west to the Persian Gulf in the east?
6. Using the map scale and a ruler, find the approximate length of the border between Saudi Arabia and the countries of Jordan, Iraq, and Kuwait.

Quiz Time

Test your knowledge of Saudi Arabia by answering these questions.

1 Which bodies of water border Saudi Arabia on the west and on the east?

2 How big is Saudi Arabia in square miles?

3 Which large desert has sand mountains 800 feet (245 m) high?

4 What species of animal became extinct in nature but has been brought back on nature reserves?

5 What is the capital city of Saudi Arabia?

6 What is the country's most important natural resource?

7 What is the official religion of Saudi Arabia?

8 In what year was the kingdom of Saudi Arabia established?

9 What is the name of the religious pilgrimage to Mecca?

10 About how many camels compete each year in the King's Cup Camel Race?

ANSWERS

1. Red Sea and Persian Gulf
2. 830,000
3. Rub' al-Khali
4. Arabian oryx
5. Riyadh
6. Petroleum
7. Islam
8. 1932
9. The hajj
10. 2,000

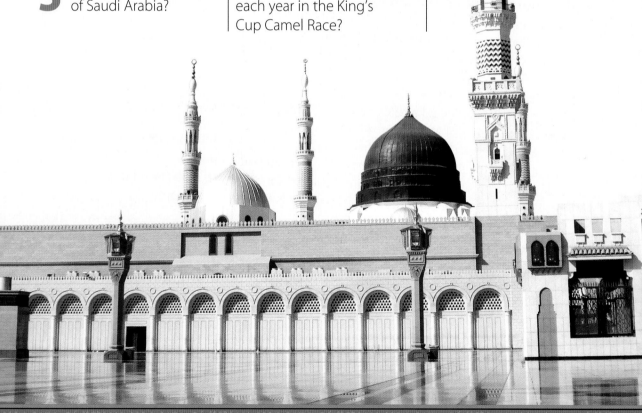

Key Words

amphibians: cold-blooded animals with backbones that live in the water and breathe with gills when young but spend at least some time on land and breathe air when adults

antiquities: objects from times long ago

archaeological: related to the study of past human life using remains such as bones, tools, or writing left by ancient peoples

calligraphy: decorative handwriting

constitution: a written document stating a country's basic principles and laws

desalination: the process of removing salt from water

descendants: people who share common ancestors

extinct: no longer found alive

GDP: gross domestic product, which is the total value of the goods and services a country or area produces

imports: brings in goods from another country

indigenous: native to a particular area

irrigation: a system for bringing water to dry areas, usually to help plants grow

life expectancy: the amount of time, on average, that a person in a certain population group can expect to live

migrate: move from one place to another at different times of year

monarchy: a form of government in which a country is ruled by a king, queen, or emperor

mortality rate: the frequency of deaths in a particular population during a specific time

nomads: people who move from place to place as a way of life

oases: areas in deserts where there is vegetation and water from a well or spring

oil reserves: deposits of oil that are known to exist and that have not yet been extracted

patriarchal: describing a social system controlled by men

peninsula: a piece of land that is almost entirely surrounded by water

petrochemicals: substances made by the processing or refining of petroleum or natural gas

pilgrimage: a journey to a holy place

plateau: an area of land that is higher than the surrounding land

species: groups of individuals with common characteristics

urban: relating to a city or town

visas: government documents allowing visitors to enter a country

Index

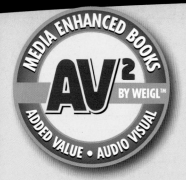

Log on to www.av2books.com

AV² by Weigl brings you media enhanced books that support active learning. Go to www.av2books.com, and enter the special code found on page 2 of this book. You will gain access to enriched and enhanced content that supplements and complements this book. Content includes video, audio, weblinks, quizzes, a slide show, and activities.

AV² Online Navigation

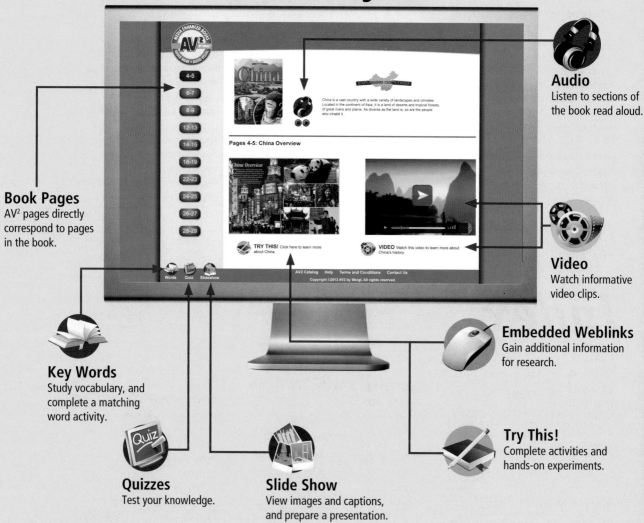

Book Pages
AV² pages directly correspond to pages in the book.

Audio
Listen to sections of the book read aloud.

Video
Watch informative video clips.

Embedded Weblinks
Gain additional information for research.

Key Words
Study vocabulary, and complete a matching word activity.

Quizzes
Test your knowledge.

Slide Show
View images and captions, and prepare a presentation.

Try This!
Complete activities and hands-on experiments.

AV² was built to bridge the gap between print and digital. We encourage you to tell us what you like and what you want to see in the future.

Sign up to be an AV² Ambassador at www.av2books.com/ambassador.